FOOTPATHS FOR FITNESS

ESSEX

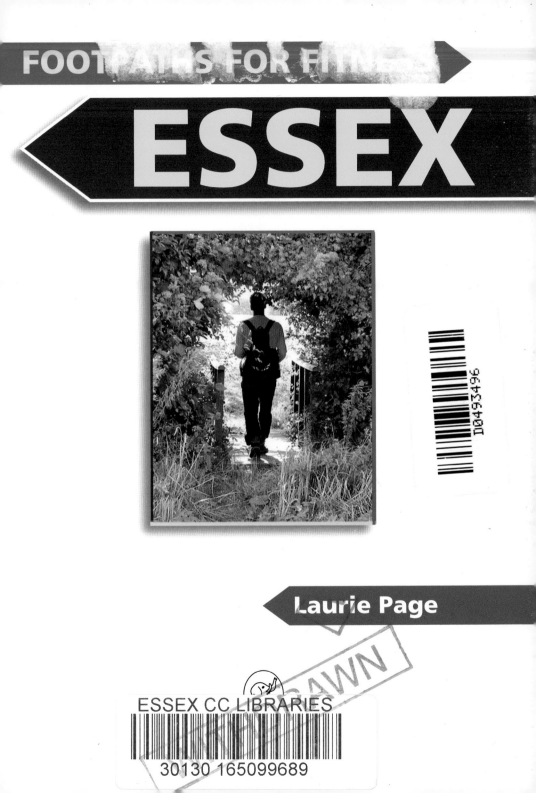

Laurie Page

First published 2009
© Laurie Page 2009

COUNTRYSIDE BOOKS
3 Catherine Road
Newbury, Berkshire

To view our complete range of books,
please visit us at
www.countrysidebooks.co.uk

ISBN: 978 1 84674 138 8

Maps by CJWT Solutions
Photographs by the author

Designed by Peter Davies, Nautilus Design
Typeset by CJWT Solutions, St Helens
Produced through MRM Associates Ltd., Reading
Printed in Thailand

CONTENTS

FOOTPATHS FOR FITNESS

FOOTPATHS FOR FITNESS **GRADE 3 – HIKE**

Introduction

Many years ago I was trained as a teacher of Physical Education and an active lifestyle has always been important to me. The ability to maintain a high level of fitness becomes more challenging as the years pass, so it was with great joy that I discovered the benefits and advantages of walking.

Still by far the most popular leisure activity for adults, there is particular enthusiasm for rambling among the older generation who find that, regardless of age, it is possible to gain enjoyment from walking and the satisfaction of keeping fit that such exercise provides. My Great Uncle Hugh wrote walking books that were published by the Great Western Railway way back in the 1930s – and he was still striding out into the countryside and writing about it in his eightieth year.

But the outdoors can be an enormous benefit to the younger generation too. It is estimated that by 2020 half of all children could be obese, and as a previous teacher of teenagers, it has been a cause for concern to me that youngsters now spend far too much time watching television or playing on the computer. Experiencing the outdoors with enjoyment and interest will go a long way to counteract the more sedentary pursuits.

However, it is not only the physical benefits of improving blood pressure and maintaining a healthy heart that matter but also the fact that walking can affect our mental fitness. Research by Natural England is now showing that the quiet and tranquillity of the countryside can lower our stress levels, improve our mood and provide more mental energy and enthusiasm. It is even suggested that it can be a genuine solution for depression.

With all this in mind, I have arranged these walks according to length (between 1½ and 6 miles) and degree of challenge (gradient, stiles and so on) in the following categories:

Grade 1 – STROLL

Grade 2 – STRIDE

Grade 3 – HIKE

If you are new to walking as an aid to fitness, I suggest that you tackle the Grade 1 walks first and progress to the more strenuous routes as your stamina improves – and all in the appealing and vastly underrated Essex countryside.

The places I visited to compile this book surprised and pleased me. There are many unspoiled villages that even most Essex people are unaware of – quiet little communities tucked away and receiving little publicity or recognition. This particularly applies to the area around Saffron Walden, where I have devised circuits starting from attractive Clavering and Arkesden, and also locations near the River Stour and the Suffolk border such as Pentlow and Lamarsh.

As usual, I have immensely enjoyed planning these routes – so much so that I have undertaken a career change and I now work at Essex County Hall as a map officer for the public rights of way team in the Highways Department. This has given me further insight into the way we provide and maintain our footpaths. 'Once a highway, always a highway' is the defining statement for our team, who work at solving the problems concerning public rights of way, and it was very gratifying to discover that most of the footpaths walked by Uncle Hugh 75 years ago still exist today and that it continues to be possible to follow the routes in his rambling books, even if the railways have disappeared!

I owe a big thank you to those who have helped me, especially my lovely lady, Linda, who has accompanied me on many of the walks and has a good eye for an appropriate photo opportunity. My aim has been to use rural rights of way and avoid roads, although on occasions a quiet country lane has been the best or the only way to go. And from time to time I have included a permissive path that is not marked on the Ordnance Survey map as a usable route. But generally these circular rambles follow the Essex footpaths, bridleways and byways and sometimes part of one of the County Trails such as the Essex Way and I hope you gain the pleasure and rewards of walking them that I did – and am continuing to do!

Laurie Page

Publisher's Note

We hope that you obtain considerable enjoyment from this book; great care has been taken in its preparation. Although at the time of publication all routes followed public rights of way or permitted paths, diversion orders can be made and permissions withdrawn.

We cannot, of course, be held responsible for such diversion orders and any inaccuracies in the text which result from these or any other changes to the routes nor any damage which might result from walkers trespassing on private property. We are anxious though that all details covering the walks are kept up to date and would therefore welcome information from readers which would be relevant to future editions.

The simple sketch maps that accompany the walks in this book are based on notes made by the author whilst checking out the routes on the ground. They are designed to show you how to reach the start, to point out the main features of the overall circuit and they contain a progression of numbers that relate to the paragraphs of the text.

However, for the benefit of a proper map, we do recommend that you purchase the relevant Ordnance Survey sheet covering your walk. The Ordnance Survey maps are widely available, especially through booksellers and local newsagents.

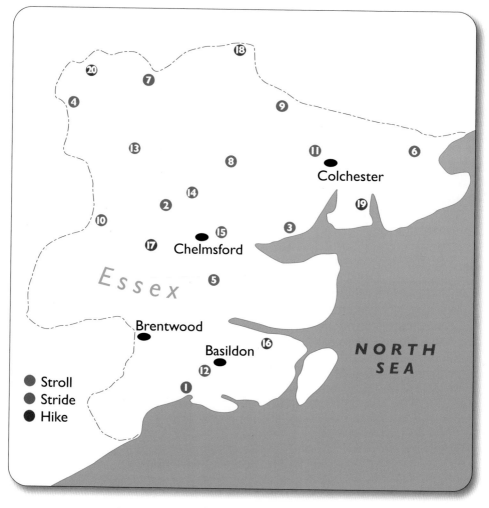

Area map showing location of the walks

Fobbing

A Village by the Thames

■ *Fobbing church at the start of the walk* ■

Sandwiched between the Thames and the town of Basildon, Fobbing has managed to retain its quaint village character. Despite being surrounded by modern builds and the oil refineries on the banks of the estuary, there is some very agreeable countryside. This short circuit contains two churches, two pubs and lakes and ponds along the way, constantly providing the walker with something of interest. Unfortunately, the churches remain locked for much of the time but they are still fascinating to visit and Fobbing parish church, St Michael's, being at the top of the hill, remains a focal point from many vantage points on the route.

> **GRADE: 1**
> **ESTIMATED CALORIE BURN: 150**

Distance: 1½ miles
Time: ¾ hour
Terrain: The paths are good but be prepared for some areas of mud near the start after heavy rain. There's a bit of a climb up the hill at the end of the walk.
Number of stiles: 5
Starting point: Outside St Michael's church in Fobbing. GR 717839.
How to get there: From the A176/A13 at the Five Bells roundabout take the road signed to Fobbing and when you reach the village, just before the road bends to the right at the White Lion pub, take the left turn into Wharf Road, a cul de sac where the church is located and park nearby. If you are going to visit the pub, you can leave your car in its car park with permission.
OS map: Explorer 175 Southend-on-Sea & Basildon
Refreshments: There are two pubs en route: the Bull in Corringham (01375 654931) and the delightful White Lion in Fobbing at the end of the walk (01375 673281).

The walk starts at the church and goes down towards the Thames plain and on through to the old part of Corringham village with its church and weatherboard houses. A good route for beginners, there is opportunity here for rest and sustenance before you return past fishing lakes to the White Lion pub in Fobbing.

1 Go down **Wharf Road**, which bends left, and about 50 yards before it terminates at the gate at the bottom there is a footpath on the right, between the houses, to **Iron Latch**. Follow the slabs of this hard path as it swings right then left to a stile. On the grass path the other side, go immediately right over another stile, following footpath number 14. This path runs parallel to the pylons on the left for a while before eventually bending away to the right and you then come to a stile at a footpath junction.

2 Go left and follow along by the wire fence, passing a large pond to the right. The route continues alongside a barbed wire fence and there are good views of the area around the Thames river plain. The path joins a wide track. Opposite the tennis courts take footpath 216 on the left but do not go over

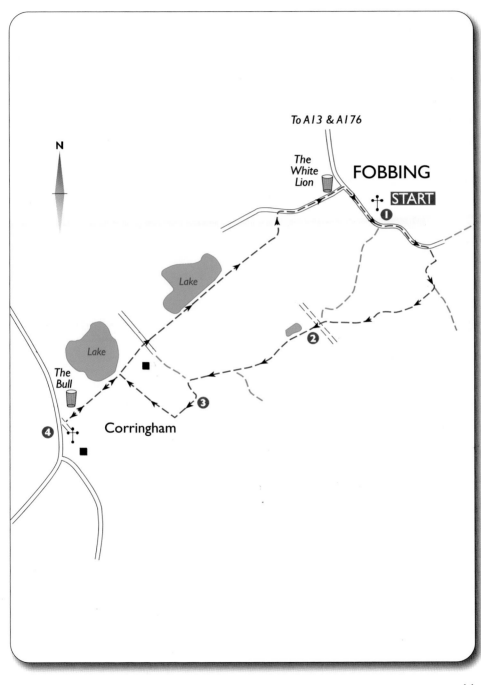

■ *The pub in Corringham* ■

the stile; instead go to the right of the stile and turn right, following along by the hedge.

3 At the end of the wire fence, turn sharp right, with a horse field to the left. When you reach the stile at the end, go straight on along a diverted path to the stile in the corner by the corrugated fence. Turn left and proceed down the alley. There is a large lake to the right. Continue to the end where you come to the **Bull pub**, **Corringham Hall Farm**, **Hall Farm Cottage** and the pretty **church of St Mary the Virgin**. You may wish to tarry awhile here.

4 Retrace your steps back up footpath 21, but continue straight on past the lake and on to the road by the school. Cross over and take footpath 22 almost opposite. This goes between fences and past another lake to the left and playing fields to the right. Proceed straight on, heading towards the church tower you can see ahead. At the concrete track, turn left and then go right at the main road. Climb uphill to the **White Lion pub** and at the junction at the top, turn right back to the church and your starting point.

2 Pleshey

A Norman Stronghold

■ *Pleshey church seen from across the fields* ■

This is an excellent route for beginners** or anyone who is returning to walking and is seeking to improve their fitness. There are no stiles or steep hills and there is an option to take a shortcut. Pleshey is a walkers' paradise with lots to see and a good network of paths in the area. It has many little thatched cottages and there is a real village feel. The Norman motte and bailey castle that stands in the centre is privately owned, but further down the street you will find a little garden that provides a viewpoint for the 'Pleshey Mount' where you can get a better idea of the height of the mound, or motte. The route traces the line of the outer bailey,

GRADE: 1
ESTIMATED CALORIE BURN: 160/180

Distance: 1¾ or 2½ miles
Time: 50 minutes or 1¼ hours
Terrain: Fairly level or very gently undulating terrain, with no difficult obstacles. This walk is best during dry weather as the ground may get a little waterlogged during rainy spells.
Number of stiles: 0
Starting point: In the main village street (simply called The Street) at the junction with Pump Lane, almost opposite the White Horse pub. GR 664144.
How to get there: From the A130 between Dunmow and Chelmsford, take the turning off westwards to Howe Street village. Pleshey is 2 miles beyond Howe Street. Go to the far end of the village and park in The Street. If you are going to visit the White Horse, you can leave your car in its car park with permission.
OS map: Explorer 183 Chelmsford & the Rodings
Refreshments: There are two good pubs in the village: the White Horse (01245 237281) near the church at the start of the walk and the Leather Bottle (01245 237291) in the centre.

with its deep ditch acting as a barrier to the village. It then follows the Essex Way along the valley, before turning back through pleasant countryside. Pleshey's beautiful parish church of Holy Trinity is an inspiring landmark during the return leg of the journey.

1 From the intersection with **Pump Lane** and **The Street**, walk up past the White Horse pub towards the church. Just the other side of the pub, take the footpath on the right. This path curves gradually round to the right, following the ditch, which is part of the ramparts of the castle bailey. When you reach the footpath junction, go over the footbridge and continue to follow the ditch. Cross the lane by the village sign and continue on to where the path S-bends past the black and white post to the road.

2 Cross the road but do not go straight on; instead, look to the left and take a path that runs along by the wire fence of the substation. This fence is soon replaced by a large open field. At the next post continue straight on or turn right to take a shortcut, continuing from point 4. If you go straight on, proceed between the ditch on the left and the field. At the next junction post take the path going to the right but now the path has the ditch to the right.

3 Go over a little footbridge into the next field and continue on until you see a wide wooden bridge over the ditch on the right without any handrail. On the other side, go right up a rutted path by the wire fence. The path bends

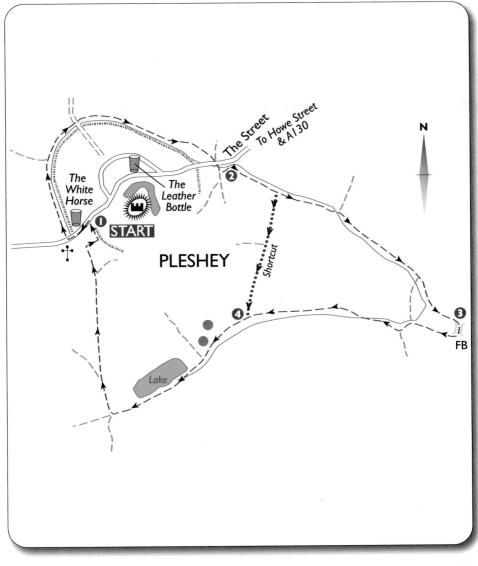

■ *Pleshey moat* ■

right then, as it bends left, turn right over the wooden bridge through the hedgerow. Bear right, keeping the ditch to the right, but at the first opportunity cross over the ditch at the opening on the right and continue along the other side of the ditch. The tower of **Pleshey church** soon comes into view. Cross another little bridge and continue to the footpath junction at the end of the field. If you have taken the shortcut, this is where you will rejoin the main route.

4 Go straight on (turn right if you have taken the shortcut) by a little wood and then pass a pretty lake on the right. When you reach the concrete track, turn right, heading towards the church. You have briefly joined the **Essex Way** but this soon branches off to the left along a grass bridleway whereas you stay on the concrete track. At the top of the slope, where it bends to the right, bear left alongside the cricket green. Take a chance to look at the church by going through the gate on the left. Otherwise follow around the edge of the cricket field to **Pump Lane**. Turn left, returning to the main street of the village.

3 Goldhanger
Down by the River Blackwater

■ *The charming village of Goldhanger* ■

The delightful village of Goldhanger, though only tiny, has a pretty church, two pubs of character and even a little agricultural museum. The cottages and houses contribute to the charm of the village, with the privately-owned Goldhanger House particularly pleasing visually.

There is something very relaxing and tranquil about water, so this route along the bank by the River Blackwater provides a calm backdrop to a pleasant short walk. The circuit starts at Goldhanger's church and continues out into some attractive countryside before running along by the river with its little creeks and tributaries and then back to the village.

17

GRADE: 1
ESTIMATED CALORIE BURN: 170

Distance: 2 miles
Time: 1 hour
Terrain: The walk is fairly flat; however, the bridges over the brooks require a little physical dexterity!
Number of stiles: 1
Starting point: In the lay-by in Head Street by the church. GR 904088.
How to get there: Goldhanger lies on the B1026 between Maldon and Tolleshunt D'Arcy. Approaching from Maldon, turn into Head Street, going into the village, and park just before you reach the Chequers in Church Street.
OS map: Explorer 176 Blackwater Estuary
Refreshments: There are two pubs in the village: the Chequers next to the church (01621 788203) and the Cricketers (01621 788468) further down Church Street. The old historic town of Maldon, with its cafés, pubs and restaurants is only ten minutes' drive away.

1 Go through the gate of the parish church and take the path to the back of the churchyard. Climb over the unusual stile at the hole in the wall, and continue along a good straight path, which runs along the edge of the field. Cross the farm track at the end of the field and proceed straight on along the edge of the meadow with a crop field on your right. At the end of this field, cross the bridge over the brook and continue up to the next hedgerow, where you turn right. Head down towards the river, keeping the hedge to your left, until you reach the complex path junction at the bottom of the slope by a footpath post.

2 Go right, passing a pond on your left, then at the next junction soon after, where the hedgerow ends, turn left, heading towards the sea wall. This is not a public right of way but a permissive path used by the local community. Proceed alongside the brook to the corner of the field. To your right you will see steps down to a little log bridge with steps back up the bank to the raised path by the river. Turn right and continue to follow the path, which bends and winds with the bank of the river. Depending on the time of year, if you need protection from a cold wind you can opt to take the parallel path at the bottom of the bank, but you will forfeit much of the beautiful view of the river. The raised path has a seat along the way as a viewpoint or for a rest. Eventually, you veer right to head back towards the church, which you will see ahead of you. Proceed to the stone steps.

3 Descend the steps to the 'River Byelaws' sign and take the path leading away from the river, which goes through the trees between the two hedgerows. Actually, there is an alternative parallel path to the left. Both end up passing the children's play area and then shortly after you reach the lane (**Fish Street**). Turn right, up past cottages and houses, to the road junction at the top by the **Chequers pub**. Turn left to the car parking area and the start.

■ *A view of the Blackwater River from Goldhanger* ■

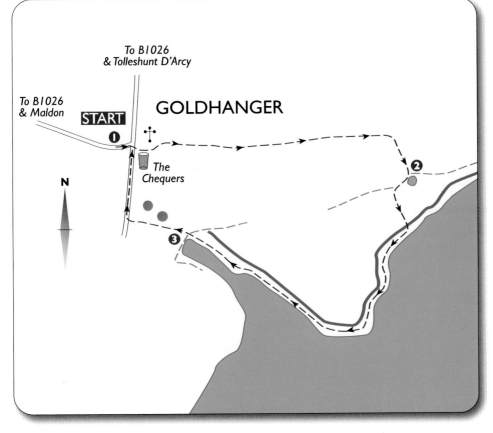

4 Clavering

Thatched Cottages All Around

FOOTPATHS FOR FITNESS

■ *The approach to the village* ■

Clavering **is one of the prettiest villages** in Essex. It has many old thatched cottages and historic houses, including the ancient guildhall. There is a magnificent parish church, rather grand for the size of the village, and the site of an old castle dating from Saxon times.

This is an easy route, just right for inexperienced walkers or those who are looking for a short excursion. From the centre of the village you set out into some beautiful open countryside, passing two old windmills along the way. These are brick-built tower mills, both without their sails; they are being converted to residential use. Then down a bridleway and back to the village via the churchyard where there is an information board about the site of the old castle by the moat. The church is open to visitors and the guildhall is through the gate on the other side of the church.

1 Go over the footbridge next to the pretty ford at the end of **Middle Street**. Walk straight over the road and up the unmarked footpath, keeping left of the '**Rossie**' house name sign, and over a stile. Then continue between the fences and over another stile and out into an open field, going gently uphill. When you reach a footpath crossroads by a telegraph pole, turn left and continue along the edge of a field with the hedge to the right, and heading towards the windmill. There is a pleasant view of lovely open countryside to the left. The path eventually emerges onto the lane by the windmill.

2 Turn left down the lane. Stay right at the fork and at the road junction by the second windmill, turn right towards **Langley**. Go downhill to the brook at the bottom, where you turn left along a bridleway. Proceed along this shaded path past the cottages. The path may be a little overgrown in places at first but it gradually improves. Continue along the tree-lined path for some distance, the bridleway eventually terminating at a lane.

3 Turn left along the lane, past an old, hidden timber-framed house. The lane bends left; further up, watch out for a footpath on the right, taking you

GRADE: 1
ESTIMATED CALORIE BURN: 170

Distance: 2 miles
Time: 1 hour
Terrain: Easy walking on good footpaths, a bridleway and some quiet lanes.
Number of stiles: 2
Starting point: By the ford in Middle Street off the B1038. GR 473319.
How to get there: Clavering lies on the B1038 between Newport in Essex and Brent Pelham in Hertfordshire. Park in Middle Street.
OS map: Explorer 194 Hertford & Bishop's Stortford
Refreshments: There are two good pubs nearby: the Fox and Hounds in the village (01799 550321) and the Cricketers at Hill Green (01799 550442), ½ mile away along the B1038 in the Newport direction.

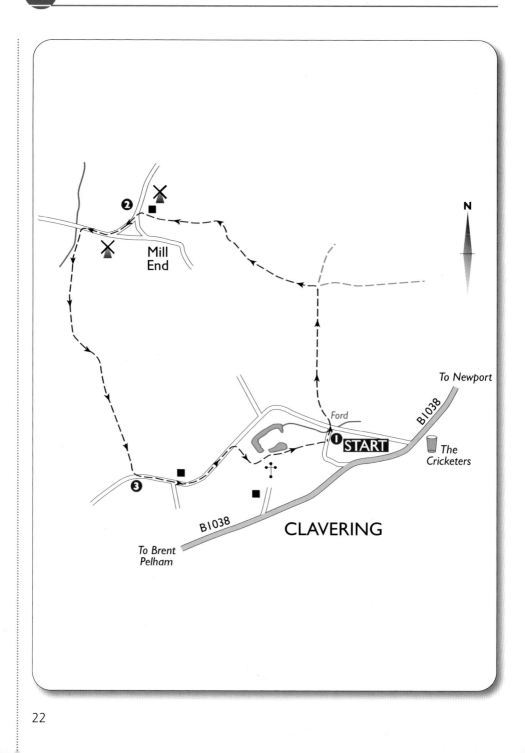

■ *Setting off at the start of the circuit* ■

over a footbridge and up a grassy path towards the church. Go through the metal swing gate into the churchyard and turn sharp left along by the fence and through the wooden gate. Follow the stony path back to the **Old Post House** in **Middle Street** and turn left to return to where you started.

5 South Hanningfield
A Countryside Oasis

■ *Looking out over the reservoir* ■

Hanningfield Reservoir, a man-made lake over 3 kilometres in width, is a large, serene stretch of water lying in the heart of the county. Completed in 1957 by building a substantial dam and pumping in water from local rivers, it now supplies over 1½ million people in South Essex. The reservoir and the area around are used for trout fishing, bird watching and, of course, for country walks! This expedition starts at what is left of the village, passes the pub, and goes through countryside, with lovely rural views, to the little parish church, returning alongside the reservoir.

FOOTPATHS FOR FITNESS

To extend the outing: from near to where the walk terminates by the pub, follow the signs to the Hanningfield Reservoir Visitor Centre about 1½ miles away to the west. Set in woodland, this offers picnic areas and walking trails and has a shop, toilets, car parking and refreshments. It is a must for bird watchers because from inside the centre there is an excellent view of the reservoir, with free binoculars and a vast colour display identifying all the British birds (01268 711001).

1 Return to **South Hanningfield Road** and turn left. At the junction with **Middlemead**, take the footpath to the right between wooden fences. This soon opens up into a little field. Cross diagonally, heading towards the left corner at the other side and out into a much larger field. Follow the hedgerow and when it ends, veer left and follow the arrow, the path cutting across the middle of the field. There are good views to both the left and right. Go gently downhill to a little wooden bridge and a stile.

GRADE: 1
ESTIMATED CALORIE BURN: 180

Distance: 2½ miles
Time: 1¼ hours
Terrain: With a number of stiles and gates to negotiate, and a testing, long but gentle uphill gradient at the end, this is a little more challenging for a walk on the short side. It is mostly on good footpaths but there is a short section along a good pavement at the beginning and end, and a very short stretch of road halfway. Towards the end, as you head towards the church after point 3, part of the route is across meadows without a defined footpath. This can be rather wet outside the summer months so take your wellies!
Number of stiles: 9
Starting point: There is a free car park overlooking the reservoir at the end of Giffords Lane. GR 738975
How to get there: At the Rettendon Turnpike (on the A130) follow the sign to the Hanningfields (Main Road). At Rettendon turn left along South Hanningfield Road. When you reach the Old Windmill pub, turn down Giffords Lane, the cul de sac almost opposite.
OS map: Explorer 175 Southend-on-Sea & Basildon
Refreshments: The Old Windmill is a very good pub near the start (01268 712280). The Hanningfield Reservoir Visitor Centre sells confectionery, snacks and teas and coffees.

2 On the other side, bear left, walking along the edge of the field with the wood to the left. As the wood ends, and you come to an opening in the hedgerow, continue straight on but now keep the hedge to your right. At the next opening, underneath the pylon wires, follow the path lined by trees on both sides. Proceed straight on but, just as the path widens, look out for the footpath post indicating a left turn over a stile/fence and alongside horse paddocks. Step through another fence and continue on down, to go over a little bridge by the brook, then back up past farm buildings to another stile. Continue straight on along the concrete path to the road.

3 Cross over and turn left along the lane. After about 100 yards turn right, taking the footpath that passes through the gate to **Romans Farm**. At the next stile soon after, bear left, going left of the pylon and along a narrow field strip to a double stile at the end. Head towards the church spire you see in the distance straight ahead. Continue uphill towards the church and the thatched house. Keep to the left at the end, taking you over another stile to the wall by the lane.

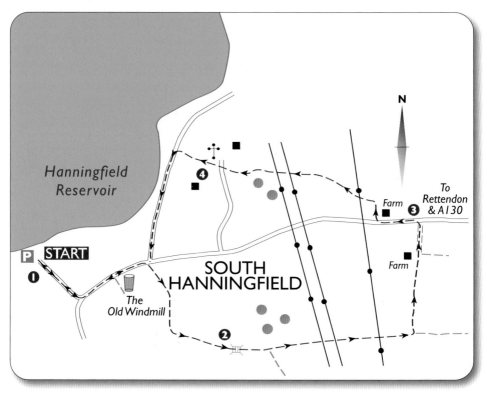

■ *An attractive dovecote seen on the walk* ■

4 Make your way to the pretty **church of South Hanningfield**. Pass by the front porch and through the graveyard to go through a white metal gate. There are good views of the reservoir ahead. On the other side of the gate, keep to the right alongside the hedge and down to the stile by the road. Turn left and use the good walkway on the other side, with pleasant views of the reservoir to your right. Continue to the road junction. Turn right along the road and then right again at the next turning, to take you back to the reservoir car park.

Great Oakley
Circling a Village

■ *The fine 18th-century Great Oakley Lodge* ■

Here is a quite straightforward walk in the Tendring district of the county, with good paths and only a smidgeon of gradient to negotiate, but the routes in the category of 'Stride' are a little longer and therefore more demanding in terms of fitness.

You will completely circumnavigate the little village of Great Oakley with farmland, country lanes, lakes and a church to enjoy along the way. You also pass Great Oakley Lodge, an attractive 18th-century building, and next to it is an airfield with two grass runways and a newly-opened clubhouse. So when the weather is fine, don't be surprised to see light aircraft coming and going quite close overhead. At the end of the walk there are some splendid views and on a clear day it is possible to see Hamford Water and Pennyhole Bay.

1 From the car park go down **Back Lane** away from the main village road and follow along a narrow passage by the high wooden fence into a field. Turn right onto the footpath that runs along the edge of the field and continue to the end, where it meets the road. Cross over to use the walkway. Turn right and proceed to the sign for **Great Oakley village**.

2 Just after the sign turn left down the footpath. Walk to the end of the field and slightly to the left, following the arrows into a residential area. Go straight on to a quiet country lane. Turn right and continue to the next road junction. Turn right up **The Avenue** and pass **All Saints' church**. At the road junction at the top, turn left and go down to the bottom of the hill by the brook.

3 Turn right along a footpath, which follows the line of the stream. Cross another brook. The path bends sharp right. Shortly after, you turn left over a concrete bridge, heading up towards **Great Oakley Lodge**. When you reach the top by the Lodge, turn right along a hard track, which passes reservoirs and then goes downhill. Just before the metal gates turn left

GRADE: 2
ESTIMATED CALORIE BURN: 360

Distance: 3¼ miles
Time: 1½ hours
Terrain: Good footpaths and quiet lanes. No steep climbs up or down.
Number of stiles: 0
Starting point: The free car park in the centre of the village on the main street. GR 194275.
How to get there: Turn off the A120 between Colchester and Harwich at Wix and drive south-east along Oakley Road. When you reach the junction with the B1414, turn left into the centre of the village.
OS map: Explorer 184 Colchester, Harwich & Clacton
Refreshments: The Maybush pub (01255 886183) at the junction of Farm Road and the High Street, close to the car park in the centre of the village.

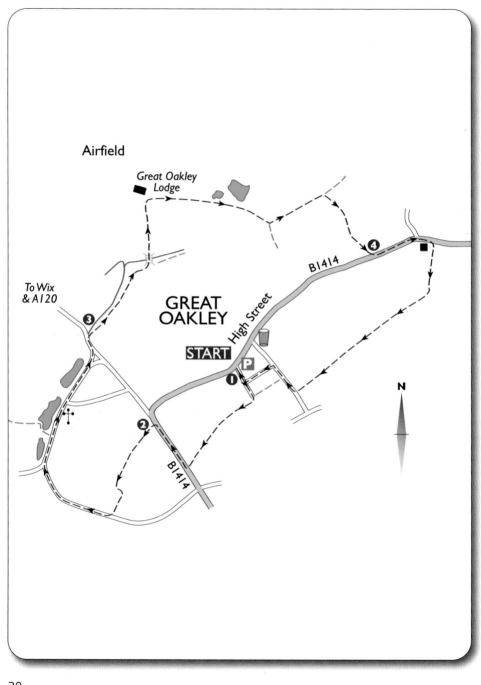

Airfield

Great Oakley
Lodge

To Wix
& A120

❸

**GREAT
OAKLEY**

START

High Street

B1414

P

❶

❷

B1414

❹

B1414

N

■ *Great Oakley church* ■

beside a field and when you reach the bridge, turn right over it, crossing the brook and going uphill. When you reach the corner of the field bear right and take the path to the road.

4 Turn left along the road past the houses. At the next junction go straight on, Very soon after, watch out for an unmarked footpath on the right next to the house called **Spurgeons Pyghtle**! Follow a good farm track, which bends right across open fields. There are distant views to the left. It seems you can pass on either side of the hedge. Continue on to the road (**Farm Road**) where you turn right, returning to the village. **Back Lane** is the next turning on the left.

7 Great Sampford
Moated Farmhouses

■ *The splendid countryside around Great Sampford* ■

There is nothing quite like a good view of the countryside and this walk provides splendid distant vistas along the way. The little village of Great Sampford lies in the heart of the north Essex countryside. The River Pant runs through it and the 14th-century church of St Michael is usually open to visitors; there are ancient wall paintings to see as well as a schoolmaster's desk from when it also served as a school. It is a very large building for such a small place because it was once the seat of a rural deanery covering 21 parishes. Already an established community, Great Sampford was granted to Battle Abbey in 1086 by William Rufus; it is mentioned in the Domesday Book during that period as Sanforda. There are a number of moated farmhouses in the area, some dating from medieval times when prosperous farmers constructed moats as status symbols.

The route weaves north and up through open country, then swings round west, then south via three successive moated farmhouses, crossing the River Pant and continuing uphill to a plateau before reaching the church and returning to the centre of the village.

1 Turn right out of **Homebridge** and walk along the main road past the Victorian school and the old village hall. At the corner where the main road veers right, turn left up **Sparepenny Lane**, going uphill past the bungalows and the thatched cottages. The lane converts to a dirt track. After the last house, look out for an unmarked footpath through the trees on the right. This path goes alongside a large field with a high hedge to the left which runs out and the path bends left through fields on both sides along a wide grass path with good views of the countryside around. At the top of the slope the footpath bends sharp left to **Howe Lane**.

2 Go straight over towards **Free Roberts Farm**, which you pass on the right. Just before the end of the lane, at the junction of paths, turn left down the bridleway. The path bends round the edge of the field. It swings right, left, then right and just as it turns left again, turn right over a stile next to the

GRADE: 2
ESTIMATED CALORIE BURN: 360

Distance: 3¼ miles
Time: 1¾ hours
Terrain: Some gentle ups and downs along quiet lanes with no traffic and some good wide footpaths.
Number of stiles: 2
Starting point: Park opposite the Red Lion Inn in Homebridge (road). GR 644354.
How to get there: Great Sampford lies at the junction between the B1053 from Radwinter to Finchingfield and the B1051 from Thaxted.
OS map: Explorer 195 Braintree & Saffron Walden
Refreshments: The Red Lion pub, which dates from 1830, at the start of the route (01799 586325).

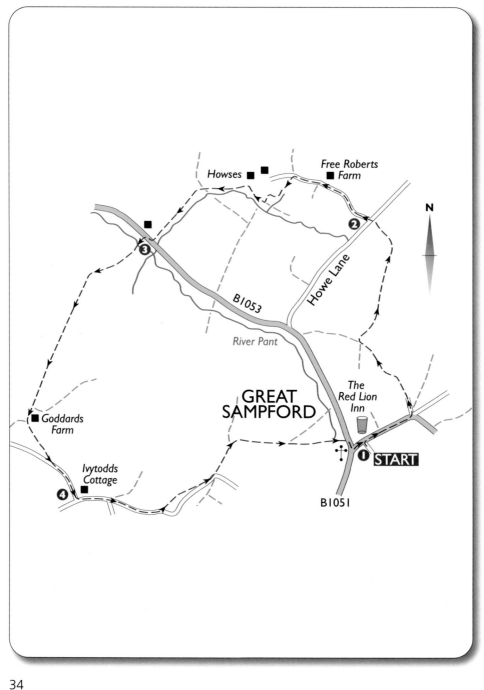

■ Howses seen from the moat ■

pond and go through a small field. Climb over another stile by **Howses** and its moat and turn left down the drive. Go over a cattle grid and continue down the tarmac drive to the road.

3 Turn right, then almost immediately left through a metal gate, along a wide grassy footpath and over a little stone bridge. The path then winds uphill between the fields. There are some glorious countryside views here. When you reach **Goddards Farm**, go past the derelict cottage with its moat and turn left just the other side, along an unmarked footpath across a field to the lane. Turn left along the tarmac lane, past **Ivytodds Cottage** with its moat and water-pump in the garden, to the road junction.

4 Turn left and at the next junction go straight on, gently downhill. At the bottom where the road turns left, you can continue along the lane or take

35

the footpath on the left just before the bend (ignore the direction of the footpath sign), which runs parallel with the road and bends right to rejoin it. Soon after, at the very next bend in the road, go straight on along the footpath that goes through the hedgerow and follows around the edge of the field. The path gradually curves right, heading towards the church. Cross the ditch by the little wooden bridge and then go over the next metal bridge. Proceed uphill and go right at the fork taking you to the church, which stands by the road junction. Go straight over to the **Red Lion pub** in the village.

■ *Great Sampford church* ■

8 *Stisted*

Beautiful Chimneys

■ *The path through the crops* ■

This quiet and relatively unknown village is just two miles from the centre of busy Braintree. There are no shops, just a pub and a pretty church. The houses in the main street display a variety of old flamboyant chimneys, mock Elizabethan and built by a local bricklayer who is buried in the churchyard. The 19th-century squire of Stisted, Onley Savill-Onley was responsible for modernising and bringing the village to its present state of glory.

The route goes from Stisted across the fields to Pattiswick, a hamlet that

37

has all but disappeared. The little church has been tastefully converted into a private residence. Then you walk back through quiet countryside and along by the golf course to the village.

1 Walk up **The Street** to the road junction opposite the **Onley Arms pub** and turn right towards **Greenstead Green**. At the next junction go straight over along the road called **Sarcel**, and at the green, bear left at the fork. In the far corner of the green you will see a footpath sign. Follow this path, which bends right and right again before turning sharp left and cutting across the middle of a large field, going uphill. At the bottom of the path, follow the footpath arrow through the trees and across a little bridge. Walk uphill through the field and at the end pass through the hedgerow and go straight on, following the farm track. This will take you to **Pattiswick Hall Farm**, where the path turns left and goes through the farm buildings and on to the lane.

2 Turn right and at the next road T-junction turn left, passing the pretty converted church and the **Old School House** next to it. Soon after, take the footpath on the left, going across the field. There is no distinct path but walk straight on towards a footpath post and then alongside a little wood that you see in the distance to your right. The path swings left and takes you to the lane. Turn left and take the next footpath right, just before the barn.

GRADE: 2
ESTIMATED CALORIE BURN: 360

Distance: 3¼ miles
Time: 1¾ hours
Terrain: Generally good paths but some cross-field tracks.
Number of stiles: 1
Starting point: The south end of The Street, by the church and in front of the teashop. GR 799247.
How to get there: Leaving Braintree, going east on the A120, take the first turning left after the Hatches Farm roundabout up Kings Lane. After 1½ miles this takes you directly into the village, where you can park on the road.
OS map: Explorer 195 Braintree & Saffron Walden
Refreshments: The teashop at the start and the Onley Arms pub (01376 325204). Near Pattiswick there is a very good pub, the Compasses (01376 561322).

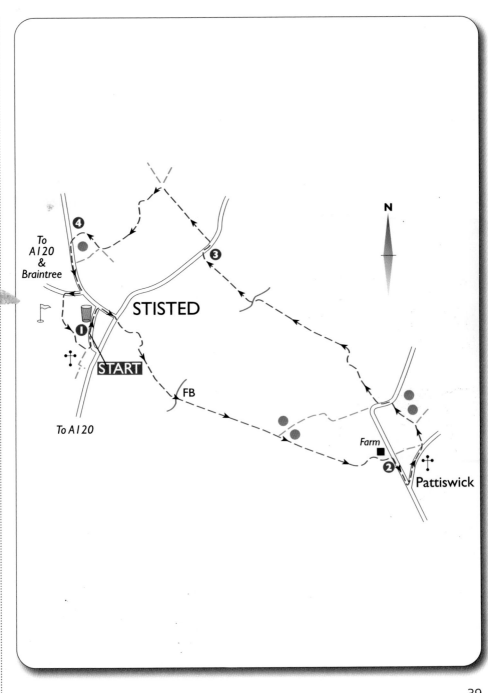

N

4

To
A120
&
Braintree

STISTED

1

START

To A120

FB

3

Farm

2

Pattiswick

■ *Attractive houses near Stisted* ■

This path turns left and follows the field boundary marked by the ditch and hedge to the right. Continue straight on at the large oak and at the bottom by the stream follow the arrow left. Shortly after, look out for the bridge on the right, crossing the brook, and follow the arrow straight on with the hedge to the right. Pass through a wooden gate. Cross the stream and head towards the cottage with the single chimney.

3 At the road turn right and then almost immediately left by the house called **Old Tan**, with its distinctive Stisted chimneys. Take the lower path, keeping the bank and ditch to the right. At the end of the field you need to go left across the open field. There is no distinct path here and you may find some heavy vegetation to negotiate. Head for the hedgerow you see in the distance. When you reach it, look out for the footpath post taking you through the hedge and a clear path on the other side leading you across the field. When you come to the footpath crossroads turn right and, as you go alongside the wood, look out for a gap through the trees on the left taking you over a planked bridge and a stile. Go through the trees and proceed past the allotments to the road.

4 Turn left towards the village and go right at the next road junction. Follow the road round to the right and shortly after **North Lodge** turn left onto a footpath. Bear left around the golf course and left again at the ninth tee, following the footpath arrow through the trees to a track, which in turn leads back to the village and the little teashop where you started.

■ *Stisted church* ■

9 Lamarsh

A Church in the Stour Valley

■ *Lamarsh church seen from the path* ■

Lamarsh is tucked away by the county border with Suffolk. The village consists of just a few houses and cottages, a pub and an unusual church with a conical-shaped tower built of flint. Lamarsh parish church of the Holy Innocents was built in Norman times and it is Grade I listed. This walk starts with quite a steady climb up a country lane and past Clees Hall to the equally remote village of Alphamstone, also with a pretty church and cottages but no pub! Then through leafy paths and, after the uphill section at the beginning of the walk, you are rewarded with a short downhill stretch at the end with a lovely view of the Stour Valley ahead and that unusual church. Both the churches that are on the route stay open and are worth a visit.

1 Turn left out of the village hall and walk along the lane. Go straight on at the first junction and up to the next junction, where, as the road bends sharp left, you turn right towards **Hornes Green**. Go quite steeply uphill for some distance. This is an early test of your fitness! Go past **Shrubs Farm**, a Victorian farmhouse built in the Georgian style, with its barn and pretty duckpond, and where the gradient is less steep. Continue on past **Specks Farm** and at **Cooks Green**, where the lane turns left, go straight on towards **Clees Hall**.

2 The lane bends right to **Clees Hall Drive** which is a bridleway closed to vehicles. Just before **Clees Hall**, where the drive bends left, follow the arrow on the footpath post, going straight on into the field. The path curves round the edge of the field, goes downhill and then S-bends through a small wooded area. Keep the trees to your left. In the corner of the field, follow the footpath arrow left through the woods. You emerge into a large meadow. Bear right, heading towards the church at **Alphamstone**. Go over the brook and back uphill to the church and the road junction. You may wish to take a little time to see the **church of St Barnabas**.

3 Take the road opposite, which is heading downhill, but go immediately left, following the footpath sign, along a stony track, through a garden. After the house bear left as far as you can, the route going between the fence and the trees. Then down some steps, through a wooden swing gate and over

GRADE: 2
ESTIMATED CALORIE BURN: 400

Distance: 3¾ miles
Time: 1 hour 40 minutes
Terrain: Good paths and a country lane; be prepared for some hills.
Number of stiles: 2
Starting point: The village hall free car park next to the church in Henny Road. GR 890360.
How to get there: Take the B1508 between West Bergholt and Sudbury. At the village of Bures turn west into Lamarsh Hill and the village is just over a mile further on.
OS map: Explorer 196 Sudbury, Hadleigh & Dedham Vale
Refreshments: The Lamarsh Lion pub in Bures Road close by, just off the route of the walk (01787 227918). It is said to have been an inn since the 14th century.

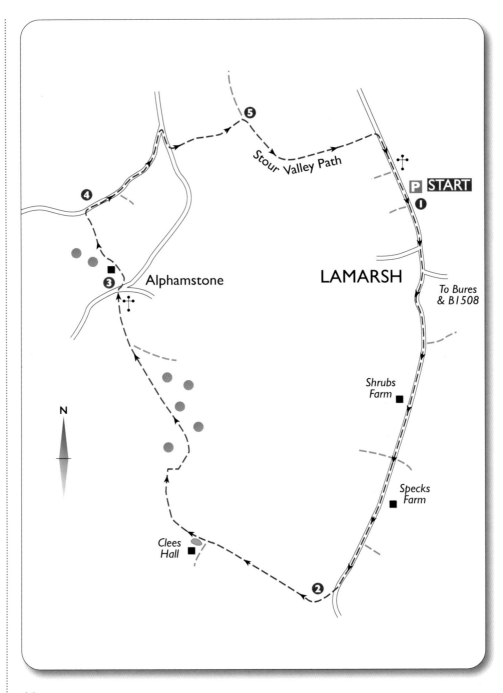

5

Stour Valley Path

P START
1

4

Alphamstone

3

LAMARSH

To Bures
& B1508

N

Shrubs
Farm ■

Specks
Farm ■

Clees
Hall ■

2

■ *The lush countryside of the Stour Valley* ■

the bridge. Proceed up to the next swing gate, taking you to a narrow country lane.

4 Turn right. The lane goes down over a brook and then there is a long stretch back uphill to a road junction. Turn right and then look out for a broken stile on the left just before the large farming sheds at **Rhyne Park Farm**. Stay right at the fork; there is no distinctive single path here but head just to the right of the line of tall trees. This brings you to a stile, which takes you out onto the **Stour Valley Path** alongside an open field with marvellous panoramic views of the Essex and Suffolk countryside ahead.

5 Turn right. The path goes along the ridge for a little way before swinging left and heading downhill towards the unusual conical-shaped church tower of the Holy Innocents in Lamarsh. Proceed to the road by **Lamarsh Hall** and turn right, going past the church and back to the village hall where you started.

10 Matching
A Divided Village

■ *The grand oak tree in Matching village* ■

You get three for the price of one on this walk as Matching appears to be a divided location with three separate village areas. The route begins at the pretty Matching Green, aptly named with its thatched cottages and houses bordering a large open green where cricket is played in the summer. The walker is then taken through some pleasant countryside to Matching Tye with a splendid pub and some interesting old dwellings, such as Gainsborough Cottage, which is dated 1692. Then on to Matching village with a magnificent oak standing outside the parish church of St Mary the Virgin and its moated manor house opposite. The route has no hills and just a few stiles at the beginning of the walk. It is very well waymarked with posts and arrows providing guidance throughout.

1 From the entrance of the **Chequers pub**, turn left along the lane by the village green to the road junction by **Elm Farm Cottage**. Take the left turning towards **Epping**. After about 100 yards, at the end of the line of conifer trees, look out for a stile on the right across a small field to two more stiles leading into a horse field. At the end of this narrow field go through the gap in the fence by the footpath post and over the little wooden bridge. Follow the yellow arrow along the edge of the field, keeping the ditch to the right. Where the ditch bends right, go straight on across the field; there may not be a very distinct path here. This will take you to a post marking a footpath crossroads.

2 Go straight on, with the dry ditch and trees to your right. At the corner of the field, go straight across the next field, heading towards the opening in the hedgerow you can see in the distance. Here there is a wooden bridge. Go straight on and turn right at the footpath post, following round the edge of the field. This will eventually take you to the road.

GRADE: 2
ESTIMATED CALORIE BURN: 420

Distance: 4 miles
Time: 2 hours
Terrain: Fairly level and easy throughout, mostly on good footpaths, with a section of road walking during the middle of the circuit, around Matching Tye.
Number of stiles: 3
Starting point: Along the road by the Chequers pub at Matching Green. GR 535110.
How to get there: From the A1060 between Bishop's Stortford and Chelmsford, turn off at Hatfield Heath onto Matching Road. Further south this becomes Downhall Road, which takes you into Matching Green.
OS map: Explorer 183 Chelmsford & The Rodings
Refreshments: There are two pubs en route: the Chequers at the start in Matching Green (01279 731276) and the Fox at Matching Tye, an old inn of character (01279 731335).

3 At the road turn left and then, as the road bends right, immediately left again down a wide bridleway, marked by a blue arrow. At the bottom of the gentle slope, bear right, keeping the hedge to your right, and continue to follow the bridleway (part of the **Forest Way** trail) around the edge of the field. This winding path eventually bends right alongside a line of tall conifers and then swings left by a farm building and on to the lane by **Willow Cottage**.

4 Turn right and at the T-junction turn right again towards **Matching Tye**. Continue on into the village. When you reach the road junction by the **Fox public house**, turn left. After about 50 yards, watch out for the turning on the right and the concealed sign for the **Forest Way** path. Keep the ditch to your right and proceed along this large field. Go all the way to the end, a distance of over ½ mile, until you reach a concrete track. Turn right towards the church. Visit if you have time.

5 Opposite the church entrance, on the other side of the track is a wooden swing gate to the next part of the route. The footpath stays close to the

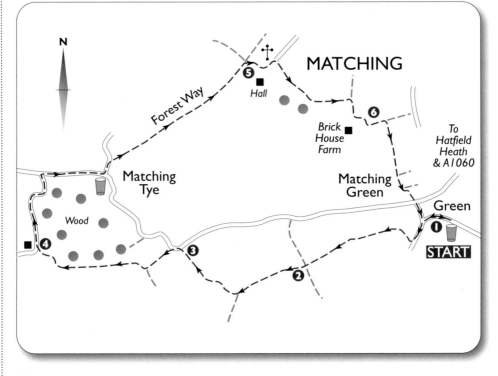

■ *The path near point 2 of the walk* ■

fence on the right side of the field. At the other end, follow the arrow pointing slightly left across an open field to the end of a little wood and then bear left, following along the grass path that cuts between the fields. This goes 90° right, then left again before the large oak, going round the grounds of **Brick House Farm** onto a tarmac track.

6 Turn left down the track. Where the hedge ends, turn right onto the footpath, going along the edge of a field and then along by a football pitch. Go left at the end of the field, then turn right along by the tall wooden fence to the road junction. To the left you will see the village green. Take the sign to **Moreton** and **Ongar** and then turn left to return to the **Chequers pub**.

Coloured Posts and the Sign of the Red Poppy

■ *Ready, steady, go!* ■

This walk goes over some pleasant rolling countryside with good views. The route sets off through the Fordham Hall Estate, which has teamed up with the Woodland Trust to plant new trees and saplings to recreate woodland; you will see these young trees along the way. The circuit is also part of some local trails, which are marked by very colourful painted posts. The walk reaches West Bergholt Old Church, which is open at weekends and well worth a visit if you have time. With Saxon origins, it has a painted wall and an old oak chest dating from about 1400. The second half of the route is along the Essex Way, marked by the sign of the red poppy and providing wide, well maintained paths. It follows along by the pretty River Colne for some distance before we leave it and return to Fordham village.

1 At the road junction by the **Three Horseshoes pub**, next to **Fordham church**, take the footpath by **Fossetts Lane** on the **Fordham Hall Estate** across a field. At the wide grass border on the other side, follow the waymarker post straight on alongside the hedge on your right to the corner of the field. Go through the gap and turn left, then immediately left again across the stout wooden bridge. Go straight ahead on the grass path, keeping the tall hedgerow and trees to the left. At the next footpath junction by the seat, turn right along the wide grass path, part of the **Fordham Hall Estate**, to the cottage at the other end.

2 Bear left, passing the house with its little pond. Turn left, heading along the grass path between the roped off fields, and then turn right at the marker post soon after, going gently downhill. At the bottom of the field follow the metal handrail to the bridge over the brook, then uphill through another metal gate and up a narrow path alongside a field to an opening by the lane.

GRADE: 2
ESTIMATED CALORIE BURN: 420

Distance: 4 miles.
Time: 2 hours.
Terrain: Almost entirely on footpaths through undulating countryside. There are some uphill sections, one quite steep, but you will find some seats for a rest along the way!
Number of stiles: 0.
Starting point: The lay-by in front of the large barn next to Fordham parish church. GR 928281.
How to get there: From the A1124 between Colchester and Halstead, at Fordham Heath turn off northwards into Wood Lane. This road bends left into Fiddler's Hill, which brings you directly to your starting point in the village after about 1½ miles.
OS map: Explorer 184 Colchester.
Refreshments: The Three Horseshoes pub in Fordham (01206 240195).

3 Turn right along the lane and at the next hedge on the left, go up the steps to a footpath running along the edge of the field. In the corner, cross the footbridge, turn right then left across a field. At the next post, proceed straight on, going downhill. Go through the gate at the bottom and turn right, following a wide path, which soon goes uphill quite steeply. Go through another metal gate and continue going uphill along a wide dirt track. This passes **Hillhouse Wood Nature Reserve** on your right. The track swings right and after some distance you will reach the church of **West Bergholt**.

4 Where the track meets the lane by the church, turn right along the lane, part of the **Essex Way**. Keep to the left at the fork, this path joining the main track further down, where the walker is able to admire some distant views of the countryside ahead. Proceed gently down the stony track to the

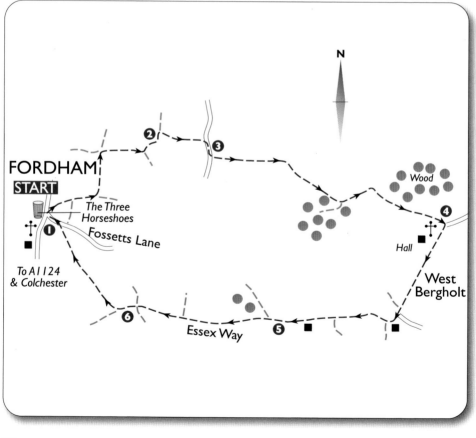

■ *West Bergholt church* ■

footpath junction. Ignore the first path on the right but take the **Essex Way** path, bearing slightly right. Keep to the right side of the barn and then continue along the track on the other side for some distance. The path swings right at a ruined house. Proceed to the concrete bridge.

5 Soon after the bridge, keep to the left track, making sure you go **left** of the large oak (the **Essex Way** arrow is hidden on the post around the corner). Keep the hedge to your right. A Second World War pillbox can be seen on the other side of the meandering **River Colne**. At the end of the field go through a metal gate and proceed straight on. At the next footpath junction, go over the bridge with the metal railings but do not cross the wooden bridge; go straight on, parallel with the river to your left.

■ *The font in West Bergholt church* ■

6 At the next footbridge turn right immediately after crossing, going uphill away from the river. Proceed straight on up to a seat and a footbridge. The church will soon come into view. Pass a reservoir on the right and continue along by a hedge and then a high wooden fence to the road. Turn left and in front of you is the pink **Three Horseshoes pub**.

Langdon Hills

Down and Up from a Country Park

■ *On the way to the Thames* ■

There is a rather surprising area south of the new town of Basildon where they have created a pleasing country park at Langdon Hills. It is so called because it is a raised hilly area to the north of the Thames plain. Starting from the hills, the route descends towards the Thames valley but if you journey down during the first half of the walk, you will have to come back up again for the second part. So this is a case of what goes down must come back up again!

1 Go to the Langdon Hills information board next to the car park. Take the hard path on the right, one of the country park walkways. This curves round to the right. At the T-junction of paths by the wire fence, turn left, going downhill. Where the path swings left, on the crown of the bend take the footpath on the right through a wooden swing gate. This is joined by a track and soon takes you to the lane called **Dry Street**.

2 Turn left and very soon, almost opposite the yellow thatched cottage, take a footpath through the gate on the right, which goes through the buildings of **Northlands Farm** with its pretty pond. Bear right down a wide grass path and over a broken stile. On a clear day it is possible to see for miles towards the **River Thames**. Proceed downhill and at the next fence, look to your right and go through the metal gate. The path goes down alongside a hedge to a wooden swing gate. Follow the field boundary as it takes you round to the right and through two more wooden gates then swings right uphill to a double gateway, a wooden and a metal gate. Go up the bank to the path in the wood.

3 Turn left and soon after, at the next T-junction of footpaths, turn right, going uphill along the wide dirt track. There are no footpath signs to help

GRADE: 2
ESTIMATED CALORIE BURN: 440

Distance: 4 miles
Time: 2 hours 10 minutes
Terrain: This is a challenging walk, almost entirely on footpaths. Although shorter in distance than some of the other routes, it has a number of stiles and some uneven ground, but it is the long uphill climb on the latter half of the walk that makes it demanding – with a steep bank at the end to try to finish you off!
Number of stiles: 9
Starting point: Langdon Hills Country Park, free car park. GR 684868.
How to get there: From the A13 at Stanford-le-Hope, take the B1007 towards Basildon. After about 2½ miles, at the top of the hill you pass the church of St Mary and All Saints on the left and just before the Harvester pub take the little service road on the right to Langdon Hills Country Park.
OS map: Explorer 175 Southend-on-Sea & Basildon.
Refreshments: The Harvester, close to the beginning of the walk (01268 544714).

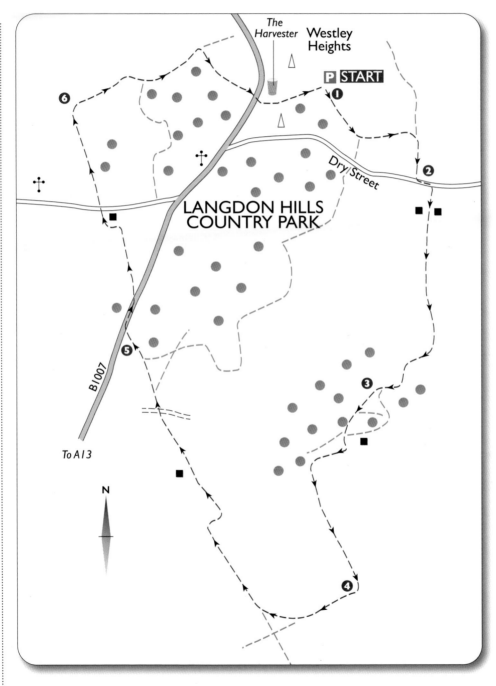

The Harvester

Westley Heights

P START

❶

❻

Dry Street

❷

LANGDON HILLS COUNTRY PARK

B1007

To A13

N

❺

❸

❹

■ *A delightful cottage in Dry Street* ■

you in this section. Continue for a few hundred yards, at first uphill before you begin to descend again. Look out for a small path on the left joining the main track. Turn left onto this narrow path, but go straight on and immediately you will find you are on the wide stony service track leading to **Briars House**, with a metal gate to your left. Walk to the right along the track, going gently down but, again, keep a sharp look out for a gap in the hedge on the left. Once through the gap, you descend down a large field towards a little wood in the distance. At the bottom you reach a footpath signpost.

4 Turn right, taking footpath 86, a narrow winding route through the woods. After about ¼ mile through the trees you come to another signpost. Go straight on, following path 32 to **Old Hill Avenue** and going over the wooden bridge and across a large grass meadow. Continue uphill with a view of the aerial mast slightly to your right. At the end of the field you are forced right alongside a wire fence, then immediately sharp left along a tree bordered path to a stile by the farm and a pretty thatched house. At the concrete track go straight over and follow path 33 to **South Hill**, going uphill. When you reach the footpath T-junction, go left and stay left at the next junction – these are woodland paths not shown on the OS map. Proceed to the top where, to your left, there is a wooden swing gate to the road.

5 Turn right and immediately cross over, taking footpath 197 on your left, over the stile and into a field where the ground may be rather uneven due to horse prints in the ground. Head towards the house you see up ahead and at the fence go left over a stile, follow alongside the wooden fence, then swing right over another stile and on up to the lane. Turn left and take footpath 154 over a stile to the right to **Langdon Hills**. Then go through a thicket and over another stile. Walk down the left side of the field. In the far corner continue over another stile and a little wooden brook crossing.

6 Turn right, admiring the views to the left and keeping **Hall Wood** to the right. If the path is not very well defined then keep to the edge of the field. Continue uphill and in the corner of the field go over the stile on the right, and take the **Wildside Walk** through the wooden gate. Go up the steep bank through the wood to the aerial mast by the road. The **Harvester** awaits to provide sustenance, or go straight on down the little road opposite to return to the car park where you started.

■ *On the route near Tilty* ■

Tucked away in this quiet corner of Essex are a few little communities, none very large and yet each with their own interesting features. Even though this walk is named Tilty, it could be called Broxted or Duton Hill. The peace of this rural area provides a contrast to the skies overhead as Tilty and Broxted lie in the shadow of nearby Stansted airport.

Because some of the footpaths around these villages may not be accessible due to overgrowth, there is a certain amount of road walking, but they are quiet country lanes and they do not detract from the enjoyment of the circuit. The route starts in the little community of Duton Hill and you soon arrive at Tilty, with its old derelict mill, ruined abbey and church that has an unusual shaped roof to its nave. Then you go west to Broxted, with another little church, and return along by a pretty river.

1 Go over the bridge to the road junction. Walk straight ahead, taking the footpath opposite, which runs along by the little stream. The path bends left by the wood to cross the stream. Go straight on by the old metal gate and as you approach the farm building, soon after the track to the left, opposite the derelict mill building, take the footpath on the left through the wooden gate. Go through the meadow past the old abbey ruins and up to a wooden swing gate by **Tilty church**. Continue past the chapel and onto the lane.

2 Turn right and follow the road past **The Grange**. After the road bends left carry on for about ½ mile and when you reach the bottom of the hill you will see a footpath on either side of the road. Take the path on the left, which goes through a field by the brook. Climb over a high stile into the next field then go through a metal gate to the next field, followed by a stile by the brook. At the end of this field, go over a stile by the road opposite **Maltings Bridge Cottage**.

3 Turn right along the road. At the next junction, go left into a driveway and then right into the field. Follow around the edge of the field, keeping the hedge to the left. When the hedgerow ends go straight on into an open

GRADE: 2
ESTIMATED CALORIE BURN: 440

Distance: 4¼ miles
Time: 2 hours 10 minutes
Terrain: A combination of footpaths and country lanes but nothing very steep.
Number of stiles: 3
Starting point: The Three Horseshoes pub at Duton Hill. GR 603268.
How to get there: From the B184 between Great Dunmow and Thaxted take the turning to Duton Hill and park in the road by the pub.
OS map: Explorer 195 Braintree & Saffron Walden
Refreshments: The Three Horseshoes pub at Duton Hill (01371 870681).

field to the telegraph wire post, where you turn right, following the line of telegraph wires all the way to the road. Turn right up the lane and at the next road junction, turn right again towards **Thaxted**. There is a seat here to rest and admire the **Old Vicarage** facing you.

4 At the next road junction turn left towards **Thaxted** and then immediately left down a footpath to **Broxted church**, which is worth a visit. Carry on to the road. Turn right and shortly after take the footpath on the left, going downhill through a crop field and then a meadow towards the post you can see in the distance. At the post go right before the bridge and follow the edge of the field to the road.

5 Ignore the footpath sign opposite but turn left along the road for a little way and you will see another footpath sign on the right on the other side

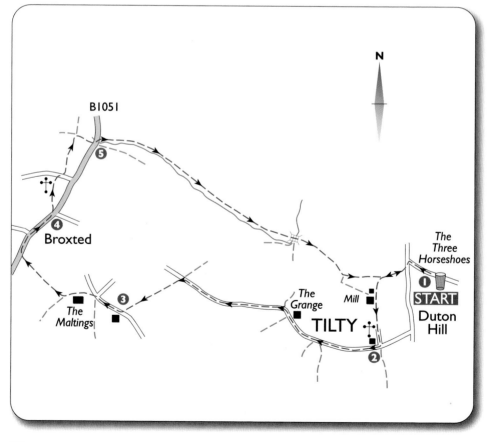

■ *The old vicarage in Broxted* ■

of the stream. Take this path and follow it alongside the stream for almost a mile. At the little stone bridge, go through the arch in the hedgerow and proceed straight on, keeping on the same side of the stream. At the next stone bridge, where the footpath forks, go left across the meadow to the post you see in the distance on the left side of the field. Follow the arrow through the trees and now retrace your steps back along the brook to the road junction at **Duton Hill**.

14 Felsted
Back to School

FOOTPATHS
FOR FITNES

■ *The stretch of river by the mill* ■

A **major feature of the village of Felsted** is its famous school and during term-time the pupils can be seen in and around the village. Just in front of the parish church, and facing the main street, is the lovely gabled building of the old school. Lord Richard Rich, who lived at Lees Priory nearby, founded it and the sons of Oliver Cromwell were pupils there. Today, the school is a magnificent building on a nearby site.

The route circles around the village, setting off south. With a wonderful view of the countryside ahead, the path descends to the Felsted's former mill and then follows a pretty stream before swinging around up to the old railway track, called the Flitch Way. Finally, you pass the unusual water tower and the grand buildings of the school to return to the centre of the village, with its historic buildings and old church.

1 From the road junction by the **Swan pub**, go down **Chelmsford Road**, past the old **Post House** and take the footpath (no 63) on the left. Go straight on to a path through the trees and then alongside the playing fields. Continue to the footpath post by the hedge at the end and turn right along the edge of the field, then go through the hedge and turn right at the footpath crossroads along a wide dirt track. This bends right to the T-junction. Turn right and continue along the farm track to the road.

2 Turn left down the road and after a few yards take the footpath on the right. This bends sharp right along the edge of a field. At the end go over the ditch and turn left by the telegraph pole. Proceed gently downhill and deviate left, then right, following the footpath arrow down towards the cottages in the distance. There is a wonderful view ahead of the surrounding countryside. At the bottom the path bends to the right of the old cottage buildings and out onto the road.

3 Turn left and just before the old mill building in front of you, turn immediately right through the wooden gates of the **Old Mill** premises. Bear immediately right again, going through the garden, over a stile and down

GRADE: 2
ESTIMATED CALORIE BURN: 520

Distance: 4¾ miles
Time: 2½ hours
Terrain: A varied route with mostly good paths and no steep gradients. One path by the river often becomes a little overgrown.
Number of stiles: 1
Starting point: The free car park next to the church. GR 676204.
How to get there: Turn off the A120 onto the B1417 east of Great Dunmow. After 2 miles you will reach the centre of the village.
OS map: Explorer 195 Braintree & Saffron Walden and a small section on 183 Chelmsford & The Rodings
Refreshments: The Swan pub (01371 820245) over the road from the car park. There are also two restaurants.

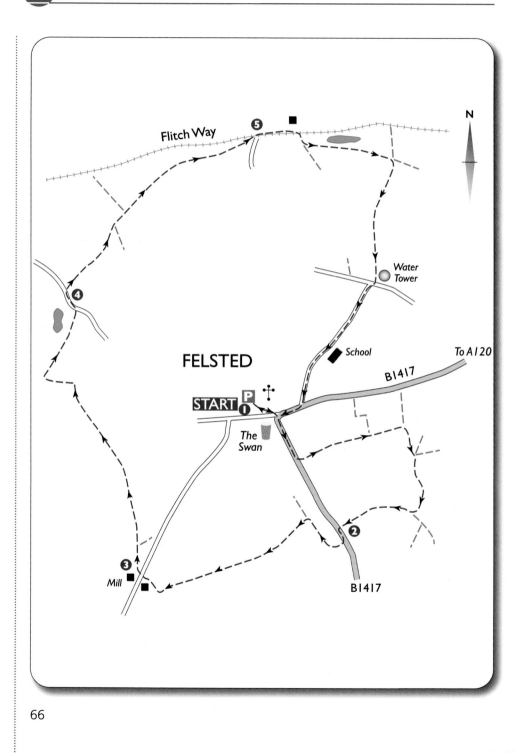

N

Flitch Way

5

Water
Tower

FELSTED

School

To A120

B1417

START
P
1

The
Swan

4

2

B1417

3

Mill

■ *The majestic buildings of Felsted School* ■

the steps to walk along by the delightful stream and past the tennis courts. Then pass through a wooden gate and continue straight on alongside the stream. Go over a little bridge and stay on the narrow path by the stream. As you emerge into an open meadow with telegraph wires above, bear left and go over the stream by the footpath (no 59) post. This takes you along a narrow path with dense vegetation on either side for some distance. Continue along by the wire fence. The path bends 90° right with the fence. Go over a bridge and carry on to the road.

4 Turn left over the bridge and shortly after the junction look out for a footpath through the trees on the right. This soon emerges into a large field. Go straight on, keeping the brook to your right, and continue into the next field. Cross the brook to your right over the bridge and go through a wooden gate into a broad meadow where you turn left, now with the brook on your left. Go through a wooden gate next to a metal gate and at the end of the next field go through another gate and up to a raised path, which is the old railway track.

5 Turn right along the railway path until you come to a footpath on the right opposite a house. Go down the slope and take the path on the left towards the lake. Bear right to walk next to the hedge, then along the edge of the field with the ditch and hedge to your left. In the next field, at the footpath post, turn right and head up towards the unusual water tower. When you reach it at the end of the field, go round the metal gate and onto the road. Go right, then immediately left at the road junction with the grass triangle. This road takes you up past the wonderful building of **Felsted School**. At the T-junction turn right along the village road and walk through the churchyard, back to the car park.

■ *The old school near the church* ■

15 *Little Baddow*
Messing About by the River

■ *Paper Mill Lock at the start of the walk* ■

The people of Little Baddow must be keen walkers, because the well trodden paths around the village are in excellent condition and the footpath signs are well displayed. There are interesting features throughout this route. You start and finish at the pretty Paper Mill Lock with its weir, boats and river trips, fishing and water activities. Along the way is the splendid 15th-century Little Baddow Hall and next to it Little Baddow church of St Mary the Virgin, which is well worth a visit – and provides a welcome resting place at a seat in the churchyard. The General's Arms is a pub of character and there is some beautiful countryside to enjoy as well as the River Chelmer. Rhododendrons were in bloom when I undertook the walk in May.

1 From the car park go up the steps to the lock, where the boats and barges are moored, and turn left, taking the path that runs along the bank of the **River Chelmer**. Follow this good path for some distance. Ignore the first footpath turning left but take the next footpath on the left, just before the blue bridge. The path goes across the middle of a large field, heading towards the church. Follow the path alongside the churchyard and go down the steps to the road.

2 Turn left along the road, but then very soon turn right up the footpath next to the wonderful pink coloured **Little Baddow Hall**. Go straight on between the buildings, then follow the footpath sign left. At the next footpath junction immediately after, turn right away from the road up a wide dirt track with an orchard to the right. Proceed straight on but before the end of the field, look out for a path on the left through the hedge; this runs between electric fences to a stile. Walk on through the trees to a bridge by the lane.

3 Turn right, going gently uphill, and where the road curves round to the right, take the footpath over the stile on the left. You still continue to go uphill

> **GRADE: 2**
> **ESTIMATED CALORIE BURN: 480**
>
> **Distance:** 4¾ miles
> **Time:** 2½ hours
> **Terrain:** The paths are wide and easy to walk but there is a long, steady uphill climb during the first part of the walk to challenge you.
> **Number of stiles:** 2
> **Starting point:** The car park at Paper Mill Lock. Parking charge at weekends in the summer season. GR 777089.
> **How to get there:** From the A414 at Danbury, take the road that runs through Little Baddow to the A12 at Hatfield Peverel. Paper Mill Lock is on the River Chelmer at the end of Little Baddow village.
> **OS map:** Explorer 183 Chelmsford & The Rodings
> **Refreshments:** The Old Stables Tea Room at Paper Mill Lock (01245 225520) and the General's Arms pub en route (01245 222069).

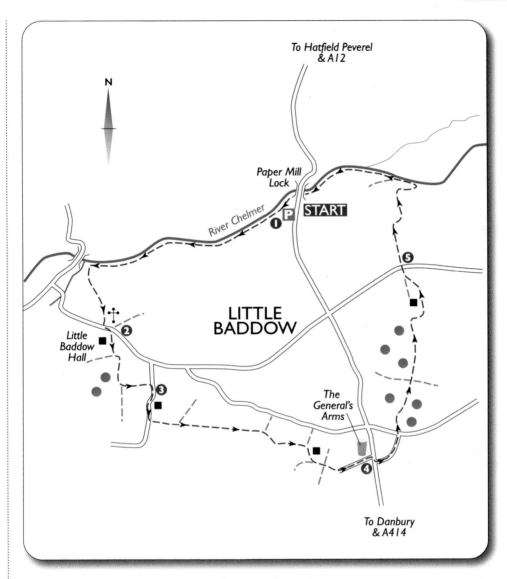

along a tree-shaded path by the fence. After a high wooden fence you reach a footpath junction. Continue straight ahead, following the yellow footpath arrow. Continue uphill past the school and then up a wide stony track to two successive footpath junctions. Go straight on at both, proceeding along a narrow tarmac road (**Parsonage Lane**), past the cricket field to the road. The **General's Arms pub** is on your left.

■ *Little Baddow Hall* ■

4 Turn right, then take the next road turning on the left, **Mill Lane**. When you reach the T-junction at the end, go straight over onto a footpath and at the next footpath junction soon after, go right towards **Old Rodney House**. Bear left at the house, going down the path next to the nature reserve. Keep to the main path close to the fence and at the footpath crossroads go downhill with a magnificent view of the countryside ahead. Descend the path by the large meadow. At the bottom by the wooden fence, turn right along a dirt track, which then bends left past the **Coach House**. Continue down a paved path and then a wide track, which bends right to the road.

5 Go straight over, taking the footpath that goes between the fields. At the bottom you are diverted right for a while but this route eventually takes you to the path by the river. Turn left and follow the path along by the water for about ½ mile. Cross the road bridge and go through the gate and back to the weir by **Paper Mill Lock**.

16 Canewdon

In Viking Country

■ Sailing boats on the River Crouch ■

Because Canewdon is located by the banks of the River Crouch, in ancient times the area was subject to raids from the Vikings, who sailed up the river in their longboats. The Battle of Ashingdon between the Saxons and the Vikings reputedly took place nearby. Today there is a good view of the river from the church on the hill and next to it has survived the old village lock up and stocks, where the rogues of the parish underwent punishment.

This walk starts at the village church of Canewdon and descends to the River Crouch where a variety of sailing boats and water craft can be seen going up and down. You then follow along the sea wall for a good distance before returning inland across the fields. The route culminates in an uphill climb to arrive back at the church.

1 Walk along the old **High Street** away from the church and back to the junction by the **Anchor pub**. Continue straight on, following the sign to **Wallasea Island**, but take the next turning on the left, **Gays Lane**. This unmade track soon provides some wonderful views of the **River Crouch** ahead. Proceed straight on ahead, downhill along the edge of a huge field. At the end of this field cross two wooden bridges and step over the gate, following the yellow arrow left across an open field towards the farm buildings. Stay to the left of a tiny pond and proceed towards the hay barn. Pass in front of the barn and just the other side turn right over a wooden gate. Go straight on to cross a stile, taking you to the river bank.

2 Turn left and follow the raised concrete path along by the river. If there is a cold wind, you have the option of following the lower path, equally as good but you will not have the privilege of the excellent views across the river. The church can be seen up on the hill to the left. After some distance the path S-bends to come closer to the river. Eventually the concrete path runs out,

GRADE: 3
ESTIMATED CALORIE BURN: 520

Distance: 5 miles
Time: 2½ hours
Terrain: You will find a perfect hard-surfaced walking track along by the river, but a testing uphill climb towards the church at the end. There is no defined path in places but you have some notable landmarks to head for.
Number of stiles: 5
Starting point: In the old High Street by the church. You can leave your car there or in Ducketts Mead, just off the High Street. GR 897945.
How to get there: Take the B1013 between Rayleigh and Rochford. At Hockley centre, go off left along Spa Road and under the railway bridge continuing into Greensward Lane and follow the road as it bends right into Ashingdon Lane. Proceed straight on at the first triangular junction and, at the next junction, go left and follow the road for about 2 miles into Canewdon village.
OS map: Explorer 175 Southend-on-Sea & Basildon or 176 Blackwater Estuary
Refreshments: There are two good pubs in the village. The Chequers Inn (01702 258251) and the Anchor Inn (01702 258213).

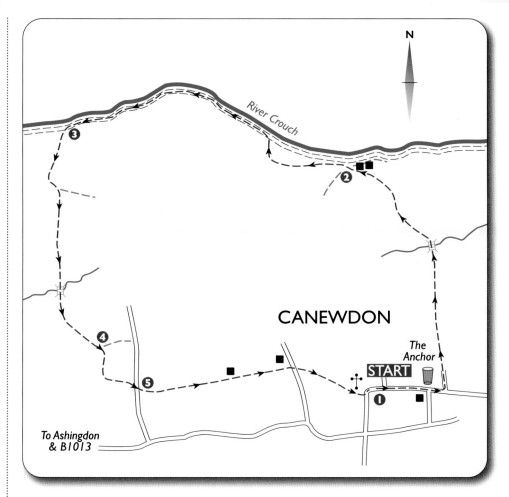

but continue along the grass path by the river. After another ¾ mile you arrive at a stile on the left.

3 Cross the stile and on the other side of the bank, join the stony track that takes you away from the river. The path swings left. Soon after, turn right at the footpath junction, leaving the main track and following the footpath arrow gently up a rough grassy track across the field. The path curves left and down to a brook. Continue straight on alongside a ditch to your left. At the end of the field follow the path through a hedge then take the bridge on the left, turning right on the other side, following the line of the brook, which is now to the right.

■ *Canewdon village church* ■

4 When you reach the corner of the field there are two options. Our route goes right over the little bridge and proceeds to the end of the field. In the corner follow the path between the wire fences, taking you to another little bridge. Turn left, following the arrows. Go through a wooden gate into the next field and at the end of this one, through a similar gate to reach the tarmac track. Turn right up the track and shortly after turn left into **Lark Hill Avenue**. This is an unmade private road and part of the **Roach Valley Way**.

5 After a while the church comes into view. When you reach the house continue straight on over a stile and across the middle of a large field. You are joined by a hedge and ditch to the left. At the concrete farm track, cross straight over into another field and go uphill directly towards the church. This footpath is a fairly steep climb that will make you puff at the top. Go through the church gate and on through the churchyard to the little village lockup and the **High Street** where you began your walk.

Blackmore
Tea at Jericho's Cottage

■ *Blackmore's village pond* ■

Blackmore is a typically quaint Essex village with a village green, a duckpond, an attractive parish church, village pubs and plenty of old houses and dwellings of character. If you have time, visit the inspiring old abbey church of St Laurence and stop at Jericho's Tea Room, which has all sorts of antiques and knick-knacks for sale.

This walk starts and finishes on the edge of Blackmore and takes in part of the St Peter's Way County Trail across the country fields, the route then swinging round the village past Paslow Green through meadows and farmland and back to rejoin St Peter's Way, which leads back into the heart of the village.

1 Follow the footpath that runs away from the main road and continues at the rear of **Green Lane**. When you reach the field by the junction with the bridleway, go straight across and head for the oak tree on the other side of the field. Just to the left of the oak tree you cross a wooden bridge and follow the waymarker right, then left alongside a ditch. At the end of the field go over a ditch and straight on towards the farm sheds you see in the distance. When you reach them, go left and at the end of the buildings turn right up the farm track to a metal gate and a waymarker post. Proceed straight on to the road.

2 Cross over and take the bridleway opposite. Bear right at the house and along a semi-shaded path through the trees and then along by a large meadow. This bends to the right and continues down between the hedges. A short way down at the waymarker post, go right along the edge of another large field with a ditch and hedge to the right. When you reach the corner of the field, follow the arrow across the footbridge and into the next field. Proceed straight on into the next field, under telegraph wires to the road by the **Wheatsheaf pub**.

GRADE: 3
ESTIMATED CALORIE BURN: 520

Distance: 5 miles
Time: 2½ hours
Terrain: Fairly level. There are a few footpaths going across open fields that are either ploughed or have no distinct line to follow, although waymarker posts will help.
Number of stiles: 2
Starting point: Green Lane, a cul de sac where you can park, off Blackmore Road at the south-west edge of the village. GR 599016.
How to get there: The village can best be reached from the A414 between Chelmsford and Chipping Ongar. Turn off into Rookery Road and after less than a mile take Nine Ashes Road on the left, which leads you directly into the village. If approaching from the east, turn off the A414 down Fingrith Hall Road to reach Blackmore.
OS map: Explorer 183 Chelmsford & The Rodings
Refreshments: There is a tea room in Blackmore at Jericho's Cottage and three pubs to choose from in the village. There is also the Wheatsheaf pub at Nine Ashes, about halfway round (01277 822220).

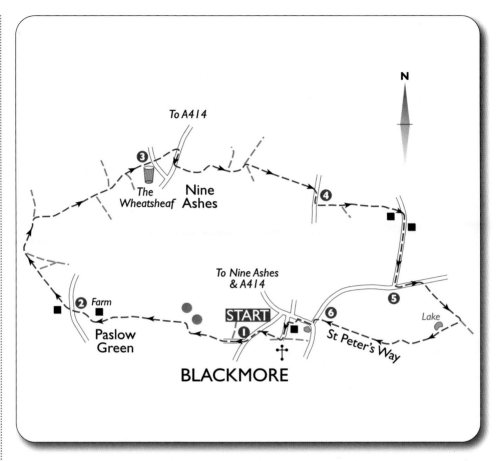

3 Take the footpath directly opposite, which leads you into a meadow and near the end go right over a wooden footbridge opposite **Rookery Cottage**. Turn right. Further up the road, look out for another wooden bridge through the trees on the left. The path zig-zags round the edge of the field and goes over a bridge where you continue straight on, going left at the next hedgerow. Keep to the hedge on the right. Further up, look for a bridge on the right taking you across a field. Go straight across past the old oaks and towards the end bear left to a gap in the hedge, which opens onto the road.

4 Turn right along the road and very soon go left over a bridge, through a swing gate and along by a grazing field. At the other end you will reach a footpath fork. Choose the left path through a field and over a stile into

■ *Friendly locals* ■

a grazing meadow. Then go over another stile and along a path heading through the farm buildings to the lane. Turn right, going down the road past **Fares** and **Russetts Cottage** and proceed to the T-junction.

5 Turn left but watch out for traffic. Further along the road, slightly concealed, is a footpath through the hedge on the right, taking you over a little bridge and into a field. Go along by the hedge but you are diverted to the other side of this further along. At the footpath junction by the path, go right across the field. Keep to the left side of the hedge, pass the lake by the post and at the next post go straight on across the field. At the next hedge bear right, taking the path that cuts across the corner of the field, then follow a grass path along by the hedge. Just past the next corner, go through the hedge and across the field to the road.

6 Turn left to a road junction and here turn right into the village. Pass the pond and the village green. Turn left at the war memorial and right at **Jericho's Cottage**. Turn left at **Church Street Cottage**, and proceed along the lane towards the parish church. Turn right at the church but then keep to the left, going through the copse and into a meadow. At the road turn left and **Green Lane**, where you started, is a little way further on the right.

■ *Blackmore church* ■

FOOTPATHS
FOR FITNES

■ *The moat surrounding Foxearth Hall* ■

The village of **Pentlow** is located in two areas, one part by the church near Cavendish and the other where you find the Pentlow Tower and the Pinkuah Arms. This pub is tucked away down a little lane and no one seems able to explain its unusual name. It is over 350 years old and it was converted from a private cottage to an alehouse. The tower, a folly that was built in the 19th century by the local minister and dedicated to his parents, acts as a significant landmark for ramblers in the area. It is now privately owned but it may be possible to arrange a climb to the top.

Starting at the car park at the Glemsford picnic site on the Essex county border with Suffolk, the route takes the walker to the little village of Foxearth, with its interesting church and manor house, and then continues along some quiet lanes followed by open countryside around Bradfield's Farm before arriving at the Pinkuah Arms – an opportunity to take some refreshment before the last leg of your journey back to the picnic site car park.

1 Turn left out of the **Glemsford picnic site** and go along the lane past the **Foxearth Fishery** to the road junction. Continue straight on ahead and up to the top of the hill. Further along, where the road bends sharply to the right, there are two footpaths. Take footpath number 21 going straight ahead and follow the line of the telegraph wires. There are good views of the surrounding countryside and **Pentlow Tower** can be seen in the distance to the right. The path eventually takes the walker over a stile and then, at the next corner of the field, left over another stile. Go straight on keeping the hedge to the left.

2 Just before you reach the road, take the footpath pointing to your right, which goes across the field and into the village of **Foxearth**. To get a good view of the **church of St Peter and St Paul**, turn right into the churchyard

---

GRADE: 3
ESTIMATED CALORIE BURN: 580

Distance: 5½ miles
Time: 2¾ hours
Terrain: Mostly good paths and a little walking along quiet lanes, particularly at the beginning of the route. There are some gentle ups and downs and a rather steeper climb near the start.
Number of stiles: 2
Starting point: The free car park at the Glemsford picnic site. GR 832464.
How to get there: From the B1064 between Foxearth and Cavendish, turn off northwards towards Glemsford. The picnic site car park is on the right after a mile. If approaching from the A1092, take the minor road signposted to Foxearth (this is just east of the B1065 turning to Glemsford); the car park is a little way down on the left.
OS map: Explorer 196 Sudbury, Hadleigh & Dedham Vale
Refreshments: The Pinkuah Arms en route (01787 280857).

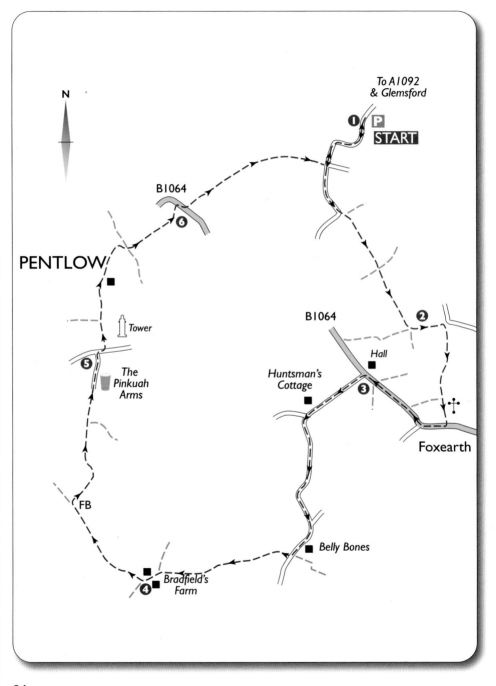

N

To A1092
& Glemsford

① P START

B1064

⑥

PENTLOW

Tower

⑤

The
Pinkuah
Arms

B1064

Hall

Huntsman's
Cottage

③

②

Foxearth

Belly Bones

FB

Bradfield's
Farm

④

■ *The Pinkuah Arms passed at point 4 of the walk* ■

and then bear left along the path by the gravestones and through the metal gate by the church tower. When you reach the B1064, turn right and follow the main road, which swings right to the moat that surrounds **Foxearth Hall**.

3 Here you turn left along the lane and at the next junction, by **Huntsman's Cottage**, proceed straight on, following the sign to the **Belchamps**. At the next junction turn right, still following the road to the Belchamps. Go past the terracotta cottage (**Belly Bones**) and soon after, where there is a footpath post on either side of the road, take the one on the right. This goes across the meadow to the gap in the hedge where there is a wooden footbridge. Then walk across the field to the next waymarker post and continue alongside a hedge and ditch and under the telegraph wires. At the post go straight across the field towards the next post and through the gap in the hedge to join the hard track going through the farm buildings and passing Bradfields farmhouse and the duckpond.

4 Stay on the main track until it takes a sharp right-angled turn to the left. Here you follow the footpath arrow straight ahead. At the next marker post go right over the bridge. At the corner of the next field go left through the hedge and over a bridge and bear left to the next post, where the path swings right, following round the edge of the field. In the corner of the field go left through the hedge. The path swings to the right and converts to a tarmac lane. The **Pinkuah Arms** pub is further down on the right.

5 Proceed down **Pinkuah Lane** to the village road and turn right, then immediately left along a footpath. (If you would like a better close-up view of **Pentlow Tower**, continue down the road a little way to the right and look through the entrance by the gate, before returning along the road and turning right up the footpath.) Walk down the lane past **School Barn Farmhouse**. When you reach the farm sheds at the bottom of the dip, just as the path curls to the left, look out for a footpath arrow on a stile to the right, taking you along a grass path. Pass the pond and go over a wooden bridge to the footpath junction. Turn right and a little way down take the next footpath on the left (the marker post is on the right), alongside a field. You are forced left over a little bridge into the next field and the footpath follows around the edge of the field to the cottages by the road.

6 Turn right and then immediately left up a bridleway by the large horse chestnut tree, between the hedgerows. After some distance, this eventually leads you to the road where you turn left, taking you back to the car park and your starting point.

■ *The Blackwater estuary is a popular spot for sailing boats* ■

Mersea Island has its busy end at West Mersea and its quiet end at East Mersea, where there are camping and caravan sites, a few farms and a country park, but almost nothing in the way of residential homes or shops. There is also Brightlingsea Reach and the Blackwater estuary to enjoy, with views of Brightlingsea town on the other side of the river and the Dengie peninsula to the south. Getting on and off the island can sometimes prove a little tricky though, as the Strood Channel, which separates Mersea from the mainland, often floods at high tide and cuts off the road. So patient waiting is required until the tide goes down.

This route takes you from the Cudmore Grove Country Park to a short stretch along the sea wall and then through some pleasing farmland to turn back along a ridge to the church, with superb views of the estuary.

1 From the **Visitor Centre car park** turn right on the footpath across the grass that leads towards the sea wall. When you reach the wall turn left and continue along the raised path that overlooks **Brightlingsea Reach**. Soon after the path bends to the left, you will see the brown signpost to the left. Come down from the sea wall path and follow the sign to '**East Mersea Road**'. Go past the house on the right and follow the stony track to the road.

2 Go straight on along the road for about ¼ mile and where the road bends sharp left, go straight ahead on the footpath over the stile by the metal gate. Then cross two more stiles and at the next one bear left along the edge of a large field. The path then cuts across the middle of the field and just before the next stile over the other side, turn right, heading across the field towards the river. In the far corner of the field, cross over the stile by the wooden gate.

3 Follow the wide, shady, tree-lined track past the thatched cottage and where the little lane bends left by **Fishpond Stables**, go straight ahead through a metal swing gate into a meadow. The route runs with the hedge and fence on the left for a short while and then cuts across the meadow and follows the fence on the right, taking you to another metal gate. Continue over a

GRADE: 3
ESTIMATED CALORIE BURN: 580

Distance: 5½ miles
Time: 2½ hours
Terrain: Mostly good footpaths although there is some uneven ground in places. Some road walking: East Road leads to a dead end and so there is little traffic but watch out for cars on the stretch by the pub (in point 5).
Number of stiles: 6
Starting point: The free Visitor Centre car park in Cudmore Grove Country Park. GR 065145.
How to get there: Take the B1025, the only road onto Mersea Island. At the fork go left, following the signs to East Mersea and continue along East Road. After the Dog and Pheasant pub take the next turning right, Broman's Lane, to the Country Park.
OS map: Explorer 184 Colchester
Refreshments: The Dog and Pheasant pub en route (01206 383206).

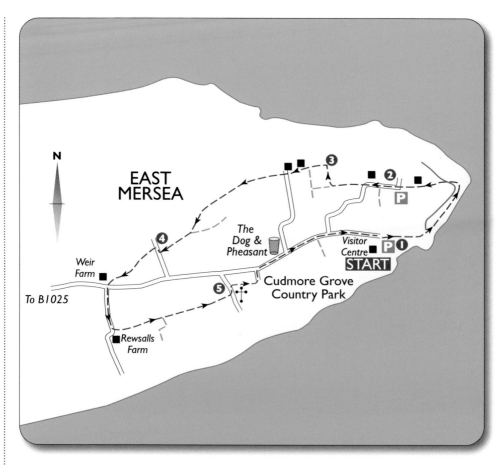

dry ditch to the next field along a wide path, keeping the hedge to your right. Go straight on into the next field along a grass path. Continue for some distance past an adjoining path to the left and on to the lane.

4 Turn right and follow the footpath sign immediately on the left. When you reach the corner of this field, bear left over the wooden bridge. The path bends gradually left and then, winding around the field, it goes left over the stile next to **Weir Farm** and on to the road junction. Cross over and go down the lane towards **Mersea Island Vineyard**. At **Rewsalls Farm**, take the footpath on the left, heading towards the church tower you see in the distance. There are good views of the sea, called **Mersea Flats**, to the right. Proceed for over ¾ mile through fields to the **parish church of East Mersea**. This is usually open if you wish to visit.

■ *A tranquil scene along the way* ■

5 Turn left up the lane and, before long, turn right at the footpath sign. This path follows the edge of the field, swinging left and terminating at the road. Turn right along the main road to the **Dog and Pheasant pub** where you may want to stop for a rest and sustenance. After passing **Shop Lane** on the left, use the grass verge and after **Fen Lane**, where the road bends sharply to the left, go right along **Broman's Lane**. This takes you back to the car park by the **Visitor Centre**.

Arkesden
Thatched Cottages and Houses

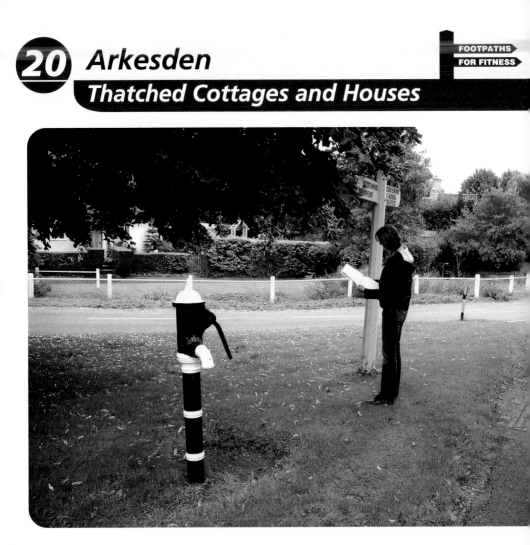

■ *Am I going the right way?* ■

If **you needed proof** that Essex can provide some beautiful countryside with pretty 'chocolate box' villages, then look no further than Arkesden. This particular area of Essex, in the north-west region of the county around Saffron Walden, provides outstanding scenery and some serene village life. Arkesden has an impressive parish church, a 17th-century thatched pub providing food of some repute, a painted waterpump, a little stream and many little thatched cottages and attractive houses.

From the centre of the village the route runs south before swinging round to the little hamlet of Rickling, then back north along a bridleway through the splendidly-named village of Wicken Bonhunt. The final leg is along the Harcamlow Way trail and back down to Arkesden. If you have a little more time to spare, this walk, which is the longest in this book, is well worthwhile.

1 From the **Axe and Compasses**, head up the road past **Hill House** and at **Parsonage Farm Cottage**, turn left up a footpath. This follows the edge of a large field with a ditch and hedge to the left. After you pass a little wood on the left, you are joined by a dirt track, which is a farm path. Keep straight on, going gently uphill, then gently back downhill to a marker post at the footpath crossroads. Turn left along a grass path next to a field. There are good views to the right and soon **Clavering windmill** can be seen in the distance. At the corner of the field the path veers sharp right with a hedge to the left. When you reach the bottom of the slope turn left and follow the corner of the field. The path swings right, then follow the footpath arrow left down a narrow fenced alley, which leads to the road.

2 Turn left along the road, then very soon after turn right down a footpath and over a stile into a field. Keep to the right and go over a second stile next to the hedge, followed by another stile next to the wooden gate, and along a wide track leading to the road. Turn right and use the walkway on the other side of the road. Soon after the end of the pavement, take the footpath left, into a large field. At the end of the hedgerow, go straight on across the

GRADE: 3
ESTIMATED CALORIE BURN: 620

Distance: 6 miles
Time: 3 hours
Terrain: There are good footpaths and bridleways and very little road walking, following a route that goes gently up and down.
Number of stiles: 5
Starting point: Park in the main village street close to the Axe and Compasses pub. GR 484344.
How to get there: From the B1038 between Newport and Clavering, turn off north-west soon after the village of Wicken Bonhunt up Poore Street. Proceed for 1 mile into the village of Arkesden.
OS map: Explorer 195 Braintree & Saffron Walden
Refreshments: The Axe and Compasses pub at the start serves excellent food (01799 550272) and you pass the Coach and Horses pub (01799 540516) en route at Wicken Bonhunt.

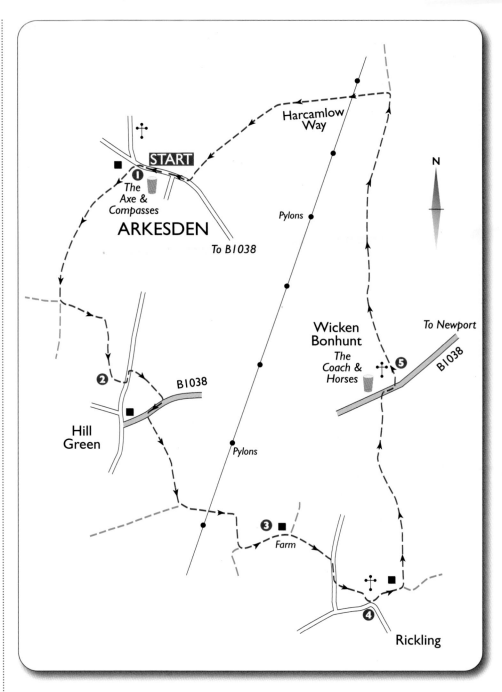

■ *The Axe and Compasses at journey's end* ■

field. Continue past the marker post and on up to the next post, where you turn left, soon passing underneath the pylons. There are good distant views of the countryside all around. At the end of the field turn right, keeping the hedge to the left. Further down, look out for the marker post and a footpath through the hedge on the left. Follow a tree-shaded path to **Coldham's Farm**, a moated house.

3 Bear right at the next marker post, away from the farm buildings and into a field. Go over a little footbridge and through a meadow of long grass and wild flowers in season, to another little planked bridge crossing, and straight on across the field to the road. Turn right along the road and when you reach the stone wall, turn left along the footpath that runs alongside it. Get over a stile to the right and then over a second stile into the churchyard and past **Rickling parish church of All Saints** (usually open if you wish to visit).

4 At the road by the triangular green, turn left up a byway and past a thatched barn. Soon after passing the thatched **Church End Farm** on the left, turn left along the public bridleway by the tall conifers. Follow a good wide path running between the fields for over ½ mile. The path swings one way and then the other, then 90° right between the hedge and the field, before turning left through a wide gap in the hedgerow towards the village of **Wicken Bonhunt**. Its church tower can be seen ahead. The path descends over the stream to the road, opposite the pink-coloured **Coach and Horses pub**.

5 Turn right and, soon after the other side of the pub, follow the bridleway on the left marked by a signpost up a wide shaded path and out into the open past a grey barn. Proceed uphill and keep to this path for over ½ mile. When you reach the marker post, turn left, leaving the bridleway, following the yellow footpath arrow (part of the **Harcamlow Way**). Pass under the pylons and through a shaded section of the path. Where the line of the tall hedge and trees ends, bear slightly left alongside a fence and then descend down towards **Arkesden village**, reaching a paved path leading to the road. Turn right and right again at the next junction, back to the centre of the village and the **Axe and Compasses pub**.

Calorie Chart

The following chart shows the approximate calories spent per hour by a person weighing 8 stone (112 lbs), 11 stone (154 lbs) and 15 stone (210 lbs)

	8 stone	11 stone	15 stone
Walking, 2 mph	160	240	312
Walking, 3 mph	210	320	416
Walking, 4½ mph	295	440	572

Note that these figures are based on moderate, not vigorous, activity.